1/06

PEOPLES OF THE
ANCIENT WORLD

Life in
Ancient
Mesopotamia

Shilpa Mehta-Jones

Crabtree Publishing Company
www.crabtreebooks.com

PEOPLES OF THE ANCIENT WORLD

Crabtree Publishing Company

www.crabtreebooks.com

For David

Coordinating editor: Ellen Rodger

Project editor: Carrie Gleason

Production coordinator: Rosie Gowsell

Art director: Rob MacGregor

Production assistance: Samara Parent

Scanning technician: Arlene Arch-Wilson

Project management assistance:
Media Projects, Inc.
Carter Smith
Laura Smyth
Aimee Kraus
Michael Greenhut

Consultants: Geoff Emberling, Director, Museum of the Oriental Institute, University of Chicago; Barbara Richman, Department of Social Studies, Farragut Middle School, Hastings-on-Hudson NY

Photographs: Bettmann/CORBIS: p. 11; Bildarchiv Preussischer Kulturbesitz / Art Resource, NY: HIP/Scala/Art Resource, NY: p. 17; (bottom), p. 28; Werner Forman/Art Resource, NY: p. 26; Werner Forman/CORBIS: p. 25; Giraudon/Art Resource, NY: p. 26; Ed Kashi/CORBIS: p. 7; David Lees/CORBIS: p. 22; Charles & Josette Lenars/CORBIS: p. 4; Erich Lessing/Art Resource, NY: p. 3, p. 9, p. 17, p. 19 p. 21; Michael Nicholson/CORBIS: p. 27; North Wind Pictures/North Wind Archives: p. 12, p. 14; Daniel O'Leary/Panos Pictures: p. 16; Gianni Dagli Orti/CORBIS: p. 5, p. 12, p. 14, p. 19, p. 21, p. 23; Scala/Art Resource, NY: p. 8, p. 24, p. 25; Shepard Sherbell/CORBIS SABA: p. 13, p. 28; Stock Montage: p. 31; Nik Wheeler/CORBIS: p. 15, p. 26. p. 30; Adam Woolfitt/CORBIS: p. 9; Michael S. Yamashita/CORBIS: p. 23; Photo CD: p. 13

Illustrations: James Burmester: p. 7, p. 19, p. 29; Roman Goforth: p. 1, pp. 10–11, p. 15; Rose Gowsell: p. 5; Robert McGregor: p. 4, p. 5, p. 6; Ole Skedsmo: p. 20, p. 29

Cartography: Jim Chernishenko: p. 6

Cover: A close up of the face of a winged lion god from Nineveh, the capital of the Assyrian empire.
Contents: The biblical story of the Tower of Babel is thought to be based on the ziggurat in the center of Babylon.
Title page: The Ishtar Gate was one set of main entrances that guarded the ancient city of Babylon.
Icon: This illustration is of a statue of a god found in a Sumerian temple. Sumerian statues often had enlarged eyes.

Crabtree Publishing Company

www.crabtreebooks.com   1-800-387-7650

Copyright © **2005 CRABTREE PUBLISHING COMPANY**.
All rights reserved. No part of this publication may be reproduced, stored in a retrieval system or be transmitted in any form or by any means, electronic, mechanical, photocopying, recording, or otherwise, without the prior written permission of Crabtree Publishing Company. In Canada: We acknowledge the financial support of the Government of Canada through the Book Publishing Industry Development Program (BPIDP) for our publishing activities.

Cataloging-in-Publication data

Mehta-Jones, Shilpa.
     Life in ancient Mesopotamia / written by Shilpa Mehta-Jones.
     p. cm. -- (Peoples of the ancient world)
     Includes index.
     ISBN 0-7787-2036-5 (rlb) -- ISBN 0-7787-2066-7 (pbk)
     1. Iraq--Civilization--To 634--Juvenile literature. I. Title. II. Series.
         DS69.5.M39 2004
         935--dc22

                                                  2004013066
                                                       LC

**Published in
the United States**
PMB 16A
350 Fifth Ave.
Suite 3308
New York, NY
10118

**Published
in Canada**
616 Welland Ave.,
St. Catharines,
Ontario, Canada
L2M 5V6

**Published in the
United Kingdom**
73 Lime Walk
Headington
Oxford
0X3 7AD
United Kingdom

**Published
in Australia**
386 Mt. Alexander Rd.,
Ascot Vale (Melbourne)
V1C 3032

Contents

Between the Rivers

The remains of ancient Mesopotamia lie between the banks of the Tigris and Euphrates rivers, in modern day Iraq. For thousands of years, people living nomadic lifestyles roamed the region in search of food. By 6000 B.C., agriculture, or the raising of crops and livestock for food, had developed. Over time, small farming settlements grew into the world's first cities.

The Birth of Civilization

Historians refer to ancient Mesopotamia as "the birthplace of civilization." The first civilization developed in the southern region of Mesopotamia, called Sumer. Here, villages grew into cities and cities grew into city-states. By about 2800 B.C., most Sumerians lived in a city-state. The city-state consisted of a central city often protected by a defensive wall, and surrounding towns and villages that depended on the city for leadership, assistance, and protection.

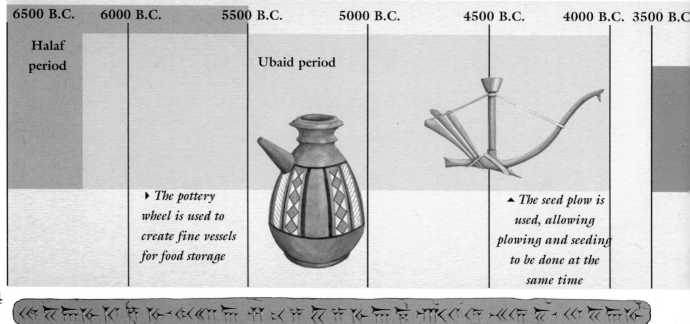

6500 B.C.	6000 B.C.	5500 B.C.	5000 B.C.	4500 B.C.	4000 B.C.	3500 B.C.
Halaf period		Ubaid period				

▶ *The pottery wheel is used to create fine vessels for food storage*

▲ *The seed plow is used, allowing plowing and seeding to be done at the same time*

◁ To defend themselves against invaders, the civilizations of Mesopotamia developed tools of war and styles of warfare, such as the wheeled chariot, bronze and iron weapons, and protective army boots for soldiers.

Center of Attention

The permanent settlements of southern Mesopotamia became a center of agriculture and trade, both for its citizens and for nomadic peoples from neighboring regions. Groups of peoples invaded and **conquered** Mesopotamia, while others settled there peacefully, and slowly gained power over time. The history of ancient Mesopotamia includes many different groups of people, conflicts, and cultural developments, such as the inventions of the wheel and writing.

◁ The name Mesopotamia comes from a Greek word that means "between two rivers."

What is a "civilization?"

Most historians agree that a "civilization" is a group of people that share common languages, some form of writing, advanced technology and science, and systems of government and religion.

3000 B.C.	2500 B.C.	2000 B.C.	1500 B.C.	1000 B.C.	500 B.C.

Persians invade
539 B.C.

Akkadian period

Sumerian period

Babylonian period

▲ *An early form of writing develops into cuneiform, or wedge-shaped symbols*

▲ *Large, stepped temples with shrines on top, called ziggurats are built*

▲ *The Ishtar Gates guard the ancient walled city of Babylon*

Assyrian period

Mountains to Marshes

The boundaries of Mesopotamia were marked by the two great rivers of the region, the Tigris and the Euphrates, and the coast of the Persian Gulf. To the north and the east lay the Zagros and Taurus mountain ranges. In the southwest, the Arabian desert bordered the rich floodplains **of the west bank of the Euphrates River. The southernmost region of Mesopotamia was a flat plain with marshes near the head of the Persian Gulf.**

The North

In the mountainous north, winters were cold and wet. Rain and snow provided water for a variety of different plants to grow. On the mountainsides, forests of oak, pine, cedar, and juniper trees gave food and shelter for wild sheep, goats, wolves, bears, hyenas, and leopards.

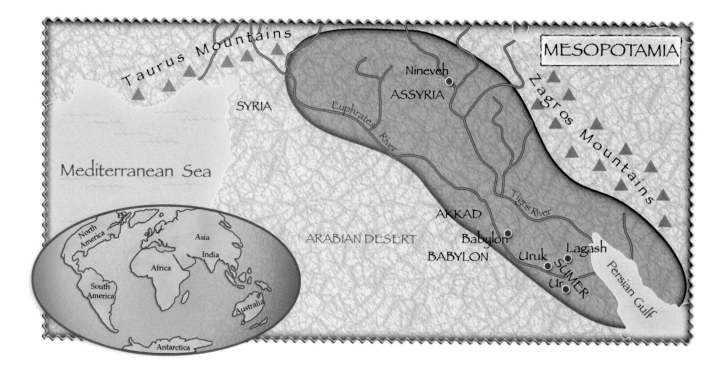

▲ *The Tigris and Euphrates emptied into the Persian Gulf 5,000 years ago. Today, the rivers meet to form a third river, the Shatt al-Arab. The flood plain is much wider today than it was in ancient times.*

Floodplains of the South

Further south, on the plain where the ancient rivers met the Persian Gulf, there was very little rain. Summer temperatures reached as high as 125° Fahrenheit (52°Celsius). Plants such as reeds and date palms grew close to rivers and streams. Further inland, the soil was dry and sandy. Many wild animals, including lions, leopards, wild cattle, boar, deer, gazelle, ostriches, vultures, and eagles, lived in the southernmost part of Mesopotamia.

Foothills and Grasslands

South of the mountains lay foothills and grassy plains. The grasslands experienced hot, dry summers that allowed for a long growing season. Less rain and snow fell in the plains than in the mountains, and hot winds blew in from southern deserts in the summer. Farmers grew grains such as wheat and barley and grazed sheep, goats, pigs, and oxen on the grassy plains.

▲ *In the northwestern Zargos, the mountains are snow-capped.*

The Life-giving Floods

The Tigris and Euphrates rivers were fed by **tributaries** that carried **silt** and soil down from the mountains. In spring, melting snow and heavy rains added large volumes of water to the rivers. The fast-flowing rivers often overflowed their banks, flooding the plains of southern Mesopotamia. The annual floods left behind the **minerals** washed down from the mountains, making the soil rich and fertile. Farmers of Mesopotamia depended on the rich soil to grow barley, wheat, and other crops.

The need for water

Farmers developed ways to water crops before they were drowned by spring floods. They used **irrigation** systems to carry water away from the rivers to ditches and canals where water was dammed, and used to water fields during the growing season. Irrigation allowed for more crops to be grown and sold, adding to the wealth of the southern region.

The Great Empires

Mesopotamia is the name given to the region where many different peoples made their homes, including the Sumerians, Akkadians, and Assyrians.

Farming Communities

In southern Mesopotamia, the earliest settlements were part of the Ubaid culture. They created small farming villages and towns and built the first temples in Mesopotamia. By 4500 B.C., Ubaid culture had spread to the north, where the farming villages of the Halaf culture already existed. People in the northern villages raised animals, grew grains, hunted wild animals, and gathered plants for food.

The Sumerians

By 3800 B.C., people known as Sumerians ruled southern Mesopotamia. Large settlements in Sumer grew into cities, which eventually became city-states. Some well-known Sumerian city-states were Ur, Lagash, and Uruk. Ur was originally an Ubaid village, but its location close to the Euphrates River made the city one of the most important trading centers by about 2500 B.C.

The Akkadians

The land of Akkad was north of Sumer. The Akkadians conquered Sumer in 2340 B.C., and united all of southern Mesopotamia under one rule. The capital city of the kingdom was Agade. By about 2125 B.C., fighting between city-states led to the collapse of Akkad. Sumerians from the southern city of Ur defeated the Akkadians and ruled southern Mesopotamia again.

The Rise of Babylon

By 2000 B.C., the Amorites, nomads from the west, had begun moving into the cities of Sumer. In time, Amorites became kings of most cities in southern Mesopotamia, including Babylon. The Hittites, warriors from the north, conquered Babylon in 1595 B.C. The Hittites left Babylon, and it fell under the rule of the Kassites, a group of nomadic people who had slowly settled throughout southern Mesopotamia. The city of Babylon was ruled by the Kassites until about 1170 B.C.

▲ *Sargon the Great led the Akkadian armies against Sumer. He was one of many great warriors from Mesopotamian cultures.*

The Assyrians

Assyria lay between Akkad and the Taurus Mountains. To the south were the more powerful city-states of Mesopotamia. Around 1100 B.C., the Assyrians began to send **military expeditions** west to control important trade routes. By 824 B.C., the Assyrians had conquered all of Mesopotamia, and had built up a large army that used iron weapons and metal armor. To keep control of the lands they conquered, the Assyrian Kings ordered the people to relocate to different areas to prevent them from **revolting** against Assyrian rule. Great palaces decorated with carved stone statues and **reliefs** showing military battles were built during the Assyrian empire.

▸ *In this carved stone relief, an Assyrian King named Asarhaddon leads the conquered by nose rings to new lands.*

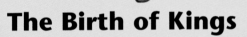

The Birth of Kings

As Sumerian civilization grew, leaders became increasingly more important. Groups of men called Councils of Elders were the first to rule city-states. The Council **appointed** temporary leaders in times of crises. A leader called an ensi was appointed to deal with agricultural problems. A lugal was chosen to lead the city's army during times of war. As **rivalries** worsened among city-states, the power of these leaders grew. By 2800 B.C., the lugals had become chief priests, lawmakers, and military commanders.

The Babylonians

The Kings of Assyria were not entirely successful in preventing revolts. By 614 B.C., different groups of people, including the Chaldeans in the south and the Medes to the east, had united to fight against Assyrian rule. Together, these groups, who came to be called the Babylonians, established a new Babylonian empire, led by King Nabopolassar. The city of Babylon was rebuilt, but the new empire was weakened by rulers who fought one another for power.

◂ *A stone statue shows Gudea, an ancient Sumerian king.*

City-states

Each city-state was independent from the others, with its own leaders, laws, and holidays. Different city-states ruled over the others at various times. Wars and agreements were made between city-states.

The City of Babylon

Babylon began as a small village in the kingdoms of Sumer and Akkad. The name Babylon comes from the word bab-ilum or babel, meaning the "gate of god." Under the Amorite kings, Babylon was a center of learning and scholarship. It became one of the greatest cities in ancient Mesopotamia.

1. People lived in houses made of mud bricks.

2. People entered the city through gates. In Babylon, there were eight main gates that surrounded the city.

3. In Babylon, the main street was called Procession Street.

4. Many city-states were protected by walls to keep out invaders.

5. Kings in city-sates built elaborate palaces and temples. In Babylon, the "Hanging Gardens," a series of lush gardens, were ordered to be built by King Nebuchadnezzar II.

6. The largest temples also included a **ziggurat**, dedicated to the main god or goddess of the city. The main god of the ancient city of Babylon was called Marduk.

10

Cities of Assyria

Nineveh, a city in the north, was the Assyrian capital. The wall that surrounded the city had fifteen main gates, each guarded by stone bull statues. Early records say that Nineveh was a beautiful city, with parks, a **botanical** garden, and a zoo.

Daily Life

The wealthiest people in Mesopotamia were government officials, professional soldiers, priests, owners of large parcels of land, and rich traders. Free citizens worked as merchants, farmers, and laborers. Free workers, or clients, were less wealthy and usually rented farmland from free citizens. There were also slaves in Mesopotamian society.

Slave Labor

Most slaves were prisoners of war captured from outside Mesopotamia. Slavery was also a form of punishment for Mesopotamians who broke the law by **assaulting** family members. Free workers could volunteer themselves or their family members into slavery to repay debts. Once their services to their owners were complete, slaves could work at other jobs to earn money. They were allowed to own property and conduct business. Some slaves made enough money to purchase their freedom.

Family Life

A Mesopotamian family was made up of a married couple and their children. Relatives lived together or close to each other. Marriages were arranged by the fathers of the bride and groom. Most men had one wife, but they had the right to marry a second wife if the first was unable to have children.

▼ *Slaves built the ziggurat in Babylon.*

◄ *The series of panels on this carved stone relief show Mesopotamians doing their daily tasks.*

Women in Mesopotamia

From childhood, girls were taught to be wives, mothers, and housekeepers, but some also became **priestesses**, poets, or even tavern-keepers. Women spun and wove cloth, ground grain, cooked, and made beverages, especially beer. Upon her husband's death, a woman fell under the protection of her husband's father or brother, or her grown son. Property was usually passed from father to son, but women could **inherit** land and household furnishings.

Food

Bread and porridge made from locally grown grains were the main foods in Mesopotamia. Barley grew well in the south, and was the most common grain. Other crops included cucumbers, onions, chickpeas, lentils, beans, and lettuce. One of the most important foods in southern Mesopotamia were dates. Dates could be eaten fresh, dried and preserved, or pressed into a syrup that was used to sweeten food and drinks. In the north, where it was too cold for date palms to grow, honey was used as a sweetener. Animals were raised and hunted for food. Goats and cows provided milk. People caught fish in rivers, streams, and swamps. Meat was sometimes boiled, but more commonly roasted or grilled. Most cooking was done in a closed domed oven or in hot ashes.

▶ *Figs were a staple of the Mesopotamian diet, along with cucumbers, onions, lettuce, and chickpeas.*

Hijab

Women often wore veils and loose clothing in Assyria. The veil distinguished respectable married women from slaves and unrespectable women, who were not allowed to wear the veil and could be punished by law for doing so. Today, many women in Iraq continue to wear the veils in public, in a custom called *hijab*.

Two veiled shoppers in Baghdad, the capital city of modern Iraq.

▼ *Barley was used to make beer. Everyone, including children, drank a weak form of beer, which was flavored with dates, honey, and spices.*

Making Cloth

Sheep's wool was an important material for making cloth. Sheep were the most common **domesticated** animal in Mesopotamia. Flax, a blue flowered plant, was also grown to make cloth. Once harvested, the flax was cleaned and combed, and then woven into a material known as linen. Linen was used to make clothes of better quality.

▲ *Assyrian men dyed and curled their beards.*

▶ *A Babylonian priest and a king in finely made clothes.*

Clothing Through the Ages

The early farmers of Mesopotamia wore clothes made of sheep or goat skins. Sumerian men often wore sheepskin skirts and short capes over their shoulders. Sumerian women wound strips of woven cloth around their bodies and draped the loose end over their shoulder. Babylonian clothing for men and women consisted of full-length, short-sleeved tunics and fringed shawls made from brightly dyed and **embroidered** wool. The Assyrians wore clothing similar to the Babylonians, but added jewelry, such as heavy gold earrings, bracelets, and necklaces. Most Mesopotamians wore leather-soled sandals with heel guards to protect their feet. Until the time of the Assyrians, even soldiers wore sandals into battle. The Assyrians introduced knee-high leather boots with soles that offered protection on rough terrain.

Homes

Free citizens lived in simple, one-story homes made from sun dried mud and straw bricks. A room with a drainage hole in the floor served as a bathroom. Each home also had a kitchen with a fireplace and cooking utensils, a **shrine** for worship, and a reception room where guests could stay overnight.

1. Ladders led to the roof, where people slept on hot summer nights.
2. Staircases overlooked the courtyards.
3. Several rooms surrounded an open courtyard. This open air courtyard let light into rooms.
4. In wealthy homes, slaves prepared meals.
5. When entering the courtyard, people washed the dirt from their feet.

▼ *Homes in the marshlands of southern Mesopotamia were made from bundles of reeds tied together, much like some are today.*

6. In wealthy homes, bedrooms were on the second floor.
7. Beds were low cots on wooden legs, or simply mats on the floor.

Economy

Mesopotamia's economy was based on agriculture. Crop surpluses **meant that people could trade food for other goods. Some people survived by trading their crafts, skills, or labor for food. Merchants and scribes emerged to keep track of transactions. Before long, trade spread among city-states.**

Agriculture

In the south, irrigation allowed farmers to bring water to their crops before the annual floodwaters came. The invention of the seed plow meant that farmers could break up the soil and plant the seeds all in one pass. The seed plow and irrigation allowed for more crops to be grown. The crops were traded as raw materials or used to make products such as oil. The most important crops were grains, such as barley and wheat. Sesame, which was eaten or used to make oil, and flax, which could be eaten, made into oil, or used for making ropes and cloth, were also grown. Dates, leeks, onions, and lentils were harvested for food.

▼ *Modern-day farmers harvesting wheat along the Tigris River, which marks the eastern edge of the Fertile Crescent. The Fertile Crescent was an area suitable for growing crops in the otherwise dry lands of the Middle East.*

Raising Animals

In northern Mesopotamia, people raised livestock such as sheep, goats, pigs, and cattle on the open meadows. Livestock provided food and materials for making leather and wool. Animals also provided a source of power to do work, allowing fewer workers to complete more work in a shorter time. Oxen were used to pull plows and wagons. Donkeys carried heavy loads on their backs and pulled carts.

Trade

The need for materials drove city-states to trade with neighboring states. When building materials such as timber and stones were needed, they had to be brought in from the mountain areas. Metal **ores** and precious stones were also brought from the mountains to make tools, jewelry, and weapons. Traders led **caravans** between Mesopotamia and the Zagros and Taurus Mountains, and even as far as Egypt to the west. Some merchants used donkey carts to carry their goods. Others used the Euphrates and Tigris rivers to ship their wares downstream.

▼ *Caravans including animals loaded with goods crossed deserts in search of trading partners.*

Money Matters

Mesopotamians originally traded through barter. Barter is a system in which one product or service is traded for another product or service of similar value. In time, bars of valuable metals, such as copper, silver, and gold were exchanged for other goods. Merchants measured these metals out in each transaction. As trade increased, it became more important to record all these transactions. Their records were written in a system called cuneiform.

▶ *The Hitties who conquered Babylon in 1595 B.C. were great traders. Through trade, the laws and ideas of Mesopotamia were spread to other lands.*

Languages

Writing first began as a system of record-keeping for administrators **and traders. In about 3500 B.C., pictographs, or shapes that represent whole words or groups of words, were etched onto clay tags and attached to bags of grain so farmers could keep track of how much grain they had. Over time, the use of pictographs changed into a written language. This writing system is called cuneiform. Cuneiform is one of the oldest known writing systems.**

Writing on the Wall

Cuneiform changed when **scribes** realized that characters could represent sounds as well as objects. Scribes started using characters that represented small words as syllables, or parts, of larger words. By stringing together three short words, the scribes could create the sound of a long word. The association between characters and sounds meant that far fewer characters were required, because there were far fewer sounds than there were objects. The rebus, a type of modern-day puzzle, also uses the sounds of words to represent syllables. Try reading the rebus below to see what it would have been like to read in ancient Mesopotamia.

U R A Gr8

Eye Bee-Leaf U R A Gr-Eight Purse-Sun
I believe you are a great person.

Writing

Cuneiform was a form of writing in which words or ideas were represented by characters made up of triangles and straight lines. The characters were pressed into wet clay tablets using a reed **stylus**. The characters represented groups of sounds, syllables, or entire words that often meant different things depending on how they were used. Cuneiform was invented by the Sumerians, but it was adopted by the Akkadians, Hittites, Assyrians, and Babylonians.

The Talk of the Town

Mesopotamia was home to many different groups of people, each with their own spoken language. The language spoken by the Sumerians is not spoken today. The Akkadians were the first Mesopotamians to speak a Semitic language, or a language belonging to a group of related languages that also includes Hebrew and Arabic. The Akkadian language changed over time. Forms of the language were used by the Assyrians, and the Babylonians. Each of these groups adapted cuneiform script slightly to its own languages.

Poetry

Poetry was an important form of spoken and written literature. The first Mesopotamian poet known by name was Enheduanna. She was a priestess and the daughter of a king. In one of Enheduanna's poems, the goddess Inanna is a ferocious warrior. In another, the poet writes about Inanna's role in ruling over civilization, as well as home and children.

The Library of Nineveh

The Assyrian king, Ashurbanipal, ordered his scribes to copy and collect cuneiform clay tablets from across the region to keep in the capital, Nineveh. This formed the first library of Mesopotamia, containing over 22,000 works, including some copies of earlier Sumerian and Akkadian texts. Ashurbanipal's collection included works on science, medicine, astronomy, religion, and folk tales. Modern researchers studying Mesopotamia use the vast Library of Nineveh as their primary source for many ancient texts.

Epic of Gilgamesh

The Epic of Gilgamesh tells the myth of Sumerian King Gilgamesh of Uruk. The stories in the epic teach lessons about the meaning of friendship, fears of sickness and death, and the search for everlasting life. Over time, these stories were collected into one long poem that was passed from one Mesopotamian civilization to another. Later civilizations added more tales and wrote new versions of others.

▶ *In the story, Gilgamesh and his friend Enkidu cut off the head of the demon Humbaba (right), guardian of the cedar forests of Lebanon.*

◀ *This example of Sumerian cuneiform script is a record of a farmer's number of goats and sheep.*

Scribes

Schools in Mesopotamia were called e-dubbas, meaning "Tablet House." Only boys were allowed to attend. The schools developed as priests began training young boys as scribes to read and write cuneiform. Students attended from sunrise to sunset, beginning in early youth and continuing into their young adulthood. They only had about six days off from school every month–three holy days and three free days. Young scribes who spoke without permission or were late for school were punished with lashes from a stick or cane.

All in a Day's Work

The first thing a young boy learned in school was how to make a clay tablet and how to hold a reed stylus properly. He memorized long lists of cuneiform symbols and the meanings of each symbol. Young scribes also learned the history of Mesopotamia, both from clay tablets that retold the events of the kings' reigns and from poetry. Scribes studied math and **astrology** so they could make calendars, and they learned law codes. Scribes learned to diagnose illnesses and to create medicine. To prepare them for life in the priesthood, young boys were taught divining, the art of reading the will of the gods, and of predicting the future.

◄ *A scribe learning to write copied cuneiform on a wet clay tablet. If he made a mistake, the clay was smoothed over and the scribe tried again.*

The Record Keepers

Once they were fully trained, scribes had an essential role in society as the recorders of facts, figures, ideas, and traditions. Many scribes worked as secretaries, book-keepers, accountants, **archivists**, recorders, and writers of hymns and epics. Some scribes sat at city gates and hired out their writing services to **illiterate** clients. In some parts of modern-day Iraq and other Middle Eastern countries, this service still exists. Other scribes in ancient Mesopotamia became doctors and diviners.

▶ *A scribe during Sumerian times was an important man because of his ability to write. Scribes were hired by people who could not read and write to write letters and record business transactions.*

The Letter of the Law

The Mesopotamian legal system was based on a collection of laws. The laws of Ur-Nammu dates back to around 2100 B.C. It consisted of 57 laws concerning crime, family, inheritance, labor, slaves, and taxes. The best known Mesopotamian collection of laws was the Code of Hammurabi. The law code was written by King Hammurabi, an Amorite king who ruled Babylon from 1792 B.C. to 1750 B.C. The code was very strict, stating the rule of "an eye for an eye, a tooth for a tooth." The 282 laws of Hammurabi's code dealt with family, labor, trade, and property. The laws were carved into eight-foot (three-meter) tall stones that were placed around the kingdom for all to see.

◀ *Hammurabi receives the code of laws from Shamash, the god of Justice.*

Religion

Religion, or the relationship between people and the gods and goddesses they worshipped, was a central part of life in Mesopotamia. The temple was at the heart of a city-state and a storehouse for the city's wealth, knowledge, and leadership. Religion was passed from generation to generation, through myths and legends about the gods and goddesses and through the traditions and duties that were held sacred in the temple.

Gods and Goddesses

The first gods worshipped in the region were believed to be in control of natural forces. The goddess of love and war was called Ishtar, or Inanna. Over time, Mesopotamians came to believe that their gods had human characteristics and would look after their city-states if they were honored in certain ways. In later Mesopotamian times, gods and goddesses were called upon by people for help and guidance. People believed that failure to honor the gods brought floods, droughts, disease, and attacks from enemies. The Mesopotamians believed that harmful spirits existed all around them, especially in deserts and ruins. These spirits rode on the wind or floated on the water, but they were not clever and could easily be deceived. People prayed to their gods for protection against evil spirits.

▲ *Mesopotamians often left carved statues and figurines of gods as gifts in the temple or buried under their houses to protect them from demons.*

Homes for the Gods

Temples, which were called the housse of the god or goddess, were a central feature of Mesopotamian cities. Each city had a protector **deity** whose temple was the largest and most prominent. Temples were part of larger complexes that included residences for priests, schools for scribes, workshops for craftspeople, and storehouses for goods. Some temples also had a ziggurat, a Mesopotamian stepped pyramid with a shrine on top, attached to them. The ziggurat was used to celebrate the New Year's festival to guarantee the fertility of the land.

Priests

Priests had special power in the community. The primary duty of priests was to honor the gods, but different groups of priests conducted different types of temple business. High priests read **omens** and advised kings. Other priests performed magic and rituals and told fortunes. Priests were also

▶ *In early Sumerian times, priest-kings lead the army and acted as go-betweens for people and their gods.*

believed to have the ability to trap evil spirits and transfer them to other animals. Priestesses, who were women, also served the gods and goddesses.

▼ *The remains of the ziggurat from the ancient Sumerian city of Ur. It is an archaeological site in present-day Iraq. The word ziggurat comes from the Akkadian word zaqaru, which means "to be high."*

Arts and Crafts

Mesopotamian potters, carvers, musicians, and metalworkers created objects of beauty to honor important gods, leaders, and historical events.

Pottery

The earliest Mesopotamian art form was pottery. Pottery was made by layering coils or slabs of clay to form bowls and jars. After about 3500 B.C., the pottery wheel was introduced. The pottery wheel was a surface that revolved as potters worked, allowing the creation of pots with thin, even sides and fancy shapes that were symmetrical. Clay was found all over Mesopotamia. Once shaped, clay vessels were usually baked in an open fire or a **kiln**.

◀ *This bowl, from about 2800 B.C., was made from limestone and inlaid with shells.*

Music of Mesopotamia

Mesopotamians invented some of the earliest known musical instruments, including the harp and the lyre. Music was composed and played to entertain royalty during feasts and gatherings. Hymns were written to praise gods and goddesses, and music often accompanied religious poems and songs. The oldest form of sheet music was carved into clay tablets. Drums and tambourines were also a part of Mesopotamian music.

The Art of Carving

Around 3000 B.C., Sumerians began to carve statues out of stone and use shells as **inlay**. They also carved decorative patterns on pottery and buildings. The most dramatic carvings found in Mesopotamia are the reliefs and statues that decorate palaces and temples. These carvings tell the story of battles or the power of kings.

▶ *This lyre, which is missing its strings, was found in the tomb of a Sumerian queen. When it was discovered, the* excavator *filled the holes where the wood once was with plaster to reconstruct the shape of the instrument.*

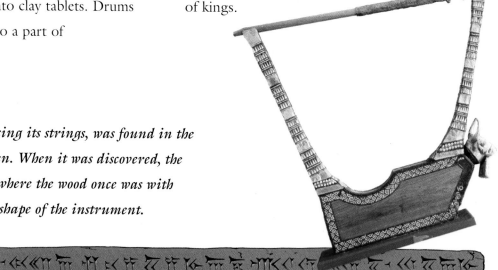

Metalwork

As cities grew and people became wealthy, demand for precious objects increased. Craftspeople began making jewelry for royalty and the upper classes. As early as 6000 B.C., Mesopotamians made objects out of hammered copper. By 4000 B.C., silver and gold came into use, and bronze in about 2500 B.C. By 1000 B.C., iron was being used to make tools and weapons. Early Mesopotamian statues of gods were made from gold, silver, and bronze. Cups, vases, harps, and lyres were also made of metal. Craftspeople spun gold and silver threads to use in handiwork. It was also common to beat metal into thin sheets and form it into shapes or stamp it with patterns.

▶ *A Sumerian princess named Pu-abi wore this elaborate headdress made with gold, silver, and a blue semi-precious gem called lapis lazuli.*

◀ *A gold helmet made by hammering the gold into the desired shape.*

▼ *This hammered metalwork adorned a palace gate in 858 B.C.*

Casting Metal

The lost wax method was used to cast metal to create several identical objects. It involved carving a model in wax and covering the wax with wet clay, leaving a small hole in the clay cover. The clay-covered model was put in an oven. The clay hardened and the wax melted, draining out the hole. The hole was then filled, and the clay became a cast into which molten, or hot liquid, bronze or glass was poured.

▼ *Sculptures of human-headed, eagle-winged bulls or lions often stood guard at entrances to Assyrian palaces and temples. The crowned head of these beasts represented supernatural power, the body stood for strength, and the wings for flight and speed.*

▲ *A reconstruction of the Ishtar Gate, one of eight gates that surrounded the ancient city of Babylon.*

The Wonders of Babylon

Mesopotamia was home to some magnificent structures. Terrace walls were built around open spaces that were filled with soil and planted with magnificent gardens. King Nebuchadnezzar II ordered the construction of the Ishtar Gate, the largest of eight entrances into the walled city of Babylon. Made from bright blue glazed bricks, the giant gateway was decorated with relief sculptures of bulls and dragons. Reliefs are carvings that are raised from their backgrounds.

◀ *The clay tablet on the far left shows early Sumerian pictographs. Next to it is a cylinder seal carved from limestone. Limestone is a soft rock that is easy to carve.*

Cylinder Seals

Mesopotamians often employed scribes to write important business documents for them on tablets of soft clay. The tablets were then "signed" by the sender by rolling a personalized cylinder seal across it. The seal was similar to a signature, and only used by the owner. Cylinder seals were used on ancient documents for about 3,000 years. The seals were rarely more than two inches (five centimeters) high. They were most often made of stone but were sometimes made of bone, ivory, glass, metal, wood, or sun-dried or baked clay. They were carved with miniature animals, gods, and other figures, as well as cuneiform characters. Very skilled craftspeople carved the design backwards, so that it would come out the right way when rolled across the clay.

▼ *Artists painted murals or used brightly colored glazed bricks and plaster to make scenes to decorate temples, palaces, and houses.*

Technology

Mesopotamians made important discoveries and inventions. These inventions and systems changed the way people lived.

Going Places

The earliest known use of the wheel was in Mesopotamia more than 6,000 years ago. The first wheels were solid, made from planks of wood shaped into discs and held together by copper or wooden brackets. They were used on carts and chariots. The Euphrates and Tigris rivers were the main trade routes of Mesopotamia. Boats carrying goods along the rivers were often built with sails. To get the boats back home, they were hauled over land by oxen.

▲ *Early chariots were very heavy and slow, but design improved with time and use. By the time of the Assyrians, chariots had spoked wheels instead of solid wheels, which made the chariots lighter and faster in war.*

◀ *In the marshes of southern Mesopotamia, small boats were made of reeds and covered in bitumen, a thick, sticky tar. Today, people in the marshes use wooden boats.*

Passing Time

The priests of Mesopotamia studied the position of the stars, the planets, the moon, and the sun, and they used this information to calculate dates and the start of seasons. The original Sumerian day was broken into 12 hours, with six hours of daylight and six hours of darkness. The new day began at sunset. The length of an hour changed to match the amount of daylight at different times of the year. The twelve-month calendar also originated in Sumer. Sumerian months were lunar, or based on the movements of the moon. Each month began with the full moon. The Babylonians later introduced the seven day week.

Medicine and Healing

A healer called an ashipu diagnosed ailments for people who were ill. Ashipu meant "conjurer" or "healer." The cause of internal diseases was thought to be the work of a god or demon. The ashipu prescribed charms and spells to drive out the spirit causing the disease. Mesopotamian surgeons performed operations on patients. The payment of a surgeon was based on the rank of his patient. Surgeons were charged a cost for making a mistake. If a surgeon saved the life of a rich person, he was paid very well. If he saved the life of a slave, he was paid only one-fifth as much. If a rich patient died during surgery, a surgeon might lose his hand, while the death of a slave cost the surgeon the price of a new slave.

Numbering Systems

Mesopotamians based their counting system on the number 60. Sixty can be divided in half (30), thirds (20), quarters (15), fifths (12), sixths (10), and tenths (6). The Assyrians used the base-60 system to become the first people to divide a circle into 360 degrees. The Mesopotamians were among the first people to use the number zero, and to use a number system for weights and measurements.

1   10

60   600

▼ *Another kind of healer, called an asu, was a specialist in herbal remedies. The knowledge of what herbs to use was written on clay tablets.*

Fall from Greatness

Mesopotamia was the most dominant region of the Middle East for thousands of years, but it was also a land of internal conflict and power struggles. Fighting among local leaders left the region vulnerable to attack. The weaknesses allowed more powerful and organized conquerors to take over the land.

The Land of Many People

Several major groups fought for control of Mesopotamia throughout its history. Some empires lasted only a few years, while others lasted for a thousand years. In all the empires, there was a constant threat of attack from outsiders.

▾ *The Persian king, Cyrus the Great, took over the city of Babylon. Persians came from present-day Iran.*

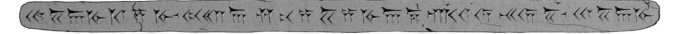

▲ *Some cities of Mesopotamia survived and became great cities of later civilizations. Hatra was built as an Assyrian city and by 100 B.C., had become a great fortified city.*

The End of an Age

After the Babylonians defeated Assyria in 614 B.C., Mesopotamia was ruled by a series of Babylonian kings who fought one another for power. There were some parts of the empire that were still loyal to Assyria. Babylon's last king was named Nabonidus. The priests of Babylon turned against Nabonidus when he ignored festivals that honored the chief god of the city, Marduk. The priests of Babylon welcomed the invasion of the Persians led by Cyrus the Great in 539 B.C. The Persian army entered the city without a fight, and Babylon became a territory in the Persian empire. By 500 B.C., all of Mesopotamia was controlled by the Persian empire.

The Salt of the Earth

Irrigation allowed for crops to be grown in many parts of Mesopotamia, but at the same time ruined the soil. When fields were flooded with irrigation water, the water was either absorbed into the soil or it evaporated into the air. If the water drained too quickly from the fields, the rich topsoil was also washed away, leaving only clay. If the water evaporated, mineral salts were left behind. As the levels of salts increased, they poisoned the plants and the fields were abandoned. When there was no crop surplus, Mesopotamians could not trade for the objects they needed to make weapons and buildings. Over time, Mesopotamians learned to deal with the salt by leaving some land unplanted for a time to allow the soil to recover.

Glossary

administrators People in charge

appointed Chosen for a position

archivist A person in charge of public records or historical documents

assaulting Violently attacking someone

astrology The study of bodies in space in the belief that they influence living things on earth

botanical Relating to plants

caravans Groups of merchants or other people traveling together on a long journey

conquered Took over by force

deity A god or goddess

domesticated Trained to live with humans

embroidered Patterns stitched in colorful threads onto fabric for decoration

excavator Someone who digs artifacts from the ground

floodplains Flat areas next to a river that frequently flood

historians People who study the past

illiterate Unable to read or write

inherit To receive money or property after someone's death

inlay To set pieces of jewels, stones, or other decoration into a surface at the same level to form a design

irrigation Supplying land with water by using ditches, human-made channels, or sprinklers

kiln An oven used to dry and harden pottery

Middle East An area made up of the countries of southwest Asia and northeast Africa

military expeditions Journeys made by an army for a specific purpose

minerals Naturally occurring, non-living substances

nomadic Moving from place to place

omens Signs of good or bad things to come

ores Rocks from which minerals can be extracted

priestess Female priests

reliefs Stone carvings in which figures are raised from the background

respectable Showing proper behavior

revolting The act of rebelling against a government

rivalry A bitter competition

scribes People who make a living by copying or recording text

shrine A religiously important place where sacred objects are kept

silt Very fine particles of dirt

stylus A sharp, pointed instrument used for writing

surpluses Extra amounts

tributaries Rivers or streams that flow into larger bodies of water

ziggurat A Mesopotamian stepped pyramid with a shrine on top

Index

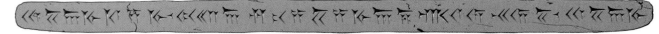